CHRISTIANITY— AND OUR WORLD

JOHN C. BENNETT

PROFESSOR OF CHRISTIAN THEOLOGY AND
PHILOSOPHY OF RELIGION
PACIFIC SCHOOL OF RELIGION

Author of
Social Salvation

Eleventh Printing

Price 50 cents

HAZEN BOOKS ON RELIGION
The Edward W. Hazen Foundation, Inc.

Distributed by
ASSOCIATION PRESS
347 Madison Avenue
NEW YORK

A Note about
The Hazen Books on Religion

THE purpose of this series is to present simply, compactly, and inexpensively a number of the best available interpretations of the Christian philosophy as a guide to Christian living today.

The series is sponsored by the Edward W. Hazen Foundation. The responsibility for selecting the titles and authors and for planning the manufacture and distribution of the volumes rests with the following committee: John C. Bennett (chairman), Wilbur Davies, Georgia Harkness, S. M. Keeny, Benson Y. Landis, Mrs. W. W. Rockwell, William L. Savage, George Stewart, Henry P. Van Dusen, and a representative of the Edward W. Hazen Foundation. The responsibility for the subject matter of the volumes rests with the authors alone.

The following twelve volumes comprise the series:

Christianity—and Our World. By John C. Bennett. (Ten printings)

Jesus. By Mary Ely Lyman. (Eight printings)

God. By Walter Horton. (Five printings)

Religious Living. By Georgia Harkness. (Eight printings)

Toward a World Christian Fellowship. By Kenneth Scott Latourette. (Five printings)

Prayer and Worship. By Douglas Steere. (Six printings)

The Church. By George Stewart. (Three printings)

Christians in an Unchristian Society. By Ernest Fremont Tittle. (Three printings)

What Is Man? By Robert L. Calhoun. (Three printings)

Christian Faith and Democracy. By Gregory Vlastos. (Five printings)

The Bible. By Walter Russell Bowie. (Three printings)

Reality and Religion. By Henry P. Van Dusen. (Three printings)

The publication of these books is a co-operative, non-profit enterprise for everybody concerned.

AUTHOR'S PREFACE

In this little book an attempt is made to interpret what Christianity as a whole means for our world. I say "as a whole" because I am convinced that we usually miss one or more of the most important elements in Christianity. I have tried to make it very clear that Christianity is a religious faith, a way of life for the individual and for society, and a movement of life—a Church.

It is hazardous to say what Christianity is because of the varied interpretations of it and the many opposing ways of life to which it has given rise. I have not tried to defend my interpretation against all comers, and I do not mean to exclude elements in Christian faith with which I have not dealt. I have emphasized those aspects of the Christian faith which seem to me to have most relevance for people who are facing the problems of our civilization. In order to see things together I have sacrificed adequacy of treatment to comprehensiveness. Other volumes in this series will provide far more adequate discussions of the specific issues raised in this volume.

I want to thank the Editor of *Christendom* for permission to use parts of an article of mine which appeared in that magazine as the basis for Chapter Two and also for permission to quote from an article by Professor William E. Hocking published in *Christendom*. Charles Scribner's Sons have kindly given per-

iii

mission for me to repeat in this book the substance of several paragraphs of my book published by them, *Social Salvation*.

Although I am alone responsible for the opinions expressed in this volume, I am greatly indebted to other members of the editorial committee for their criticisms and suggestions.

Auburn Theological Seminary,   J. C. B.
   October 1, 1936.

CONTENTS

INTRODUCTION

Christians of the post-war generation are called upon to make harder decisions than were their parents. For the past generation it was possible to be sincerely Christian and yet fit easily into civilization. The world seemed to be a hospitable place for the development of Christian faith and the realization of Christian ideals. Those who saw clearly the real conflicts between Christianity and the world were able to hope that the world was being transformed according to a Christian pattern. It did seem possible to decide for Christianity without deciding against major trends in civilization.

One of the most prophetic Christian spirits of the past generation, and also one of the most realistic, was Walter Rauschenbusch. In 1912 he wrote a book entitled *Christianizing the Social Order*. In that book he indicated that the greater part of the work of Christianizing the social order was already done. Already we had largely succeeded in Christianizing the home, the church, the school, and the political state. Now, he suggested, we face the last great conquest, the conquest of the economic order; and within a measurable time we shall have what can be called a Christian society. Rauschenbusch was not blind to the real dangers which threatened those hopes, and he admitted that we could never have more than an approximation to a Christian society; but in his hopes he spoke for his generation in America. I quote him, not to hold him up to criticism, but to indicate that the wisest Christians of the pre-war generation saw ahead of them no enduring conflict between Christianity and their world.

Today, such an outlook is completely foreign to the world in which we live. No longer can Christians fit easily into their world, not even with the help of high expectations for the immediate future. The forces which have most momentum in our society are pagan forces. Sometimes they are avowedly anti-Christian. Sometimes they are indifferent to Christianity. Where there is a Christian veneer what lies behind it sometimes seems more opposed to Christianity than the most blatant atheism. Some forms of fascism which do lip service to Christianity are more hostile to what Christianity means than communism. On every continent the lines are being drawn sharply. Christianity is coming to mean something more definite against a background of opposition. It is becoming more provocative, and in calling for harder decisions it is more clearly worthy of our loyalty.

In this book an attempt will be made to suggest some of the definite things which Christianity does mean for our time. Those aspects of it will be stressed which are in clearest relation to the most serious problems which we face. There are four such problems which will be discussed. The first is the organization of life apart from God, on a completely secular basis. The second is the moral confusion which has followed the disintegration of the authoritarian morality of the churches. The third is the economic system which controls so many areas of our lives and yet which has grown up almost completely without guidance or check from Christian ideals. The fourth is the rise of the tyranny of the fascist state combined with narrow nationalism, racialism, and the threat of war.

It would not be true to say that Christianity within itself provides a solution for all those problems. The situation is less simple than that. But, this book is written out of the conviction that in the face of those problems Christianity says the things which need most to be said.

CHAPTER I

CHRISTIANITY AND SECULARISM

I shall use the word "secularism" for that characteristic of our world according to which life is organized apart from God, as though God did not exist. In using that word and in dealing first with the subject of secularism I want to warn against the view which is quite popular in the churches that our chief task is to combine all the religious resources of the world against secularism. (Unethical religion is a far greater danger to true religion than secularism.) It is possible to be closer to God in seeking what God wills while denying his existence than in defending an unjust order of things while praising him. And yet, secularism is a great distortion and impoverishment of human life.

There are two things which secularism means. From a religious point of view it means that the highest objects of devotion are human ideals and human causes which emerge in the social process.) It is in practice very easy to single out one such ideal or cause and make a god of it. The most significant forms of secularism are not those which have grown out of academic skepticism, but those which with religious enthusiasm make a god of the nation or of the communist utopia. From the point of view of the interpretation of life secularism implies an answer to the final question which life forces us to ask—what is the nature of the reality to which we owe our existence? Its answer (dressed up as it may be in various forms) is that man is the product of a blind cosmic process (or processes)—a blind process which does not know what it is producing, which does not know the difference between good and evil, beauty and ugliness, persons and things.) It matters little whether we think of this process in mechanical terms or in vitalistic terms: the result is essentially the same.

This secularism has at least three roots in our society. It is rooted in our intellectual life. Our one-sided emphasis upon science tends to level down the world to those things with which the sciences deal most successfully. A reaction is setting in against this tendency, but our minds have been largely formed by the scientific habit of selecting from the world those aspects of it which fit the purpose of science and of suggesting that they are the only sure reality. The development of a public educational system in this country separated from all forms of religion in order to prevent any one form of religion from dominating it has created a bias of mind to which religion seems to have no organic connection with the major interests of the educated man. The persistence beyond their time of forms of religion in the churches which are incompatible even with the assured results of science and which are an affront to the consciences of men who have been exposed to the scientific spirit has greatly aggravated these tendencies.

But more important than the intellectual roots of secularism are some of the habits of living which go with our kind of civilization. Our lives are so cluttered with things that it is not strange that there has

been some atrophying of our spirits. We are so con-
stantly stimulated by speed and noise and entertain-
ment and crowds that quiet and reflection are almost
beyond attainment. The results of applied science
have been so amazing and have so completely made
over the externals of our lives that we have become
preoccupied with human achievements. There has
come over us what critics of our culture have called a
sense of "human autonomy" or "self sufficiency." Also,
there has been the inevitable specialization, which has
meant that many of our best minds (as well as those
who must specialize in what seems meaningless drudg-
ery) spend their lives in concentration upon one small
segment of the world from which they can get little
light concerning the meaning of life as a whole.
Strengthening all of these factors is the nature of city
life, which again reminds us of what man has built
and cuts us off from the world of nature, without which
men lose their sense of ultimate dependence upon
what is more than human.

One further root of secularism must be mentioned
because it is so different from the others. This is the
antireligious bias of the radical social movements in
many countries, and especially of communism. In
part this is a reflection of the secularism of our civilization. But it is also in part a judgment upon religion
as it has been lived; a judgment which is too much
deserved. There is no doubt but that religious institutions have been controlled by the groups with
most privilege in society, that religion has been very
often an opiate of the people—an opiate alike for the

consciences of the exploiters and for the feelings of the exploited. The revolutionary criticism of society which is implicit in Christianity has generally been soft-pedaled. So, in the Soviet Union all the force of education and social approval is thrown against religion in spite of the fact that religious worship is tolerated. There are signs that this tendency is being moderated, but already the attitudes of a whole generation have been molded. For the first time in history the masses, as well as the sophisticated few, deliberately reject not only all true religion but even all supernatural superstition. It is one of the tragedies with which Christians have to live that authentic elements of Christianity are embodied in a movement which has turned against all religion, and that churches which are being punished because they lack those same elements of their faith readily assume that they serve Christ by denouncing the secularism of radicalism instead of by changing their own ways of life. There is, however, a growing minority in the churches which understands that this root of secularism cannot be cut except by an inner transformation of the churches themselves.

What Christianity Means

Over against this secular interpretation of life outlines of the Christian faith stand in sharp relief, and overshadow in their importance the differences of belief among Christians. I shall here present an interpretation of Christianity in contrast to secularism in the form of a modern creed.

It is the Christian faith that there is nothing which is worthy of our supreme devotion short of the reality upon which we and the whole structure of our lives ultimately depend. Whatever else is true of God, God is more than human, prior to man, the being to which we owe our existence. Christians may differ about the degree to which God transcends the known universe, how far he is revealed in it, how far he is present within it; but God is not merely another word for the universe. The universe depends upon God and not God upon the universe.

It is the Christian faith that men in their search for the meaning of their lives cannot stop short of God. They need God as the intellectual explanation of their existence as well as for the sense of belonging to an order of things which gives coherence to their experience.

It is the Christian faith that God is the final source of moral obligation. One of the surest facts of human life is the fact that moral demands are made upon us which we cannot refuse without the sense of having somehow fallen. The significance of these demands is obscured when they happen to coincide with our interests or desires, or with what our social group approves. It is when a moral demand cuts across our own desires and interests and runs counter to the approval of our group that we are forced to raise the question: Why is this demand binding on me? Notice that we are not here concerned with the origin of the particular thing which is demanded. It may have developed through a long process of trial and error in social experience. The question here is not, What is the good? but rather, Why should I bother about the good? It is in the answer to that question that morality and religion meet. Here more surely than anywhere else we feel within our own souls the impact of a demand which derives its authority from beyond ourselves and from beyond society. To disobey is to fall, and to fall not merely in our own eyes or in the eyes of society. There are some words of Professor Hocking which put with great effectiveness what I have just been saying:

"The day is saved, if it is saved, by men who keep on working for a group which is not worthy of their effort, frequently under the calumny and attack of those they are best serving. The day is saved by men who keep on, longer than any collectivity can require them to keep on.

"The essence of the matter is this—and I rest the case on it [the case for the significance of religion]. There is such a thing as conscience; what is it? Not a racial memory, but a sense of obligation that lights on this or that course when reflection has detached us for a moment from the clamor of self-interest. Is conscience a luxury, a psychological accident, an economic lubricant, an ephemeral sentiment induced by an indifferent world? Or is it a companionship, an intimation of destiny, a perception that human choices have some bearing upon an eternal order of being? To suppose that in some way conscience represents the nature of things makes all the difference in a man's life; to have such men as its components makes all the difference in the life of a civilization." *

It is the Christian faith that God is personal. That word is a stumbling block to many of our contemporaries. What it means can be put in this way. In

_____
* *Christendom*, October, 1936.

the nature of the case God is unique. One cannot describe God by comparing him with anything else of the same kind. The most that we can do is to find suggestions or symbols in the world of our experience (the only world which is open to us at all) which seem fruitful in our thought about God. The possibilities among such suggestions are very limited. To say that God is personal is to say that God is more like a person than like a thing, more like a person than like a machine, more like a person than like a mathematical proposition, more like a person than like a tree. This last suggestion is pertinent, because the whole conception of God as blind life-urge is symbolized quite well by a tree. But, when we use the word "personal" as a description of God, we mean to include only a few of the characteristics of persons. Our human limitations which are inherent in our physical existence obviously do not apply to God. Those characteristics which do apply to God are: *awareness, intelligence, purposiveness, the capacity to appreciate, the capacity to respond to persons.* It is difficult to see how a God who lacks those qualities could be a fitting object of devotion or an adequate explanation of existence, or one to whom our conduct could make any difference.

It is the Christian faith that in Jesus Christ we have the surest clue to the nature of God. It is not enough to say that God is personal. That might leave it open to believe that God has the characteristics of a Napoleon or a Mussolini—the man of power. To say that it is in Christ-like personality that we have a true symbol of the nature of God becomes especially significant when we contrast Jesus with other types of persons. Moreover, God is revealed not only in the personality of Jesus but also in his teaching about God and in his religious response to God. His trust in God and his commitment to God form the clearest portrayal of man's right relationship with God.

It is the Christian faith that it is the purpose of God that the spirit of Jesus should be the norm for our lives, and that men should develop in the world a fellowship which knows no barriers of race or class or nation, and which is characterized by abundance of life, mutual loyalty, and a common devotion to God. So long as Christians take seriously the revelation of God and of his purpose which they find in Jesus they have a corrective for the most menacing perversions of our time, for racialism and nationalism, for economic injustice and war.

It is the Christian faith that there is a judgment of God which can be observed in personal life and in the events of history. God seeks to draw us, to persuade us, but we can resist him; and when we resist him too stubbornly we find ourselves up against punishment. This punishment is at work in the moral structure of things which makes evil in the long run self-defeating. In the next chapter will be shown more clearly the nature of this moral structure. It is enough to stress here that through it we can discern the sterner side of God's activity. Men who organize their lives around the narrow self or one or two impulses of the narrow self find themselves in blind alleys. The world is unable permanently to organize its life on the basis of injustice and nationalism without reaping chaos and conflict which become each year more destructive. But one of our grounds for hope is that the prospect of the judgment of God upon us or the foretaste of the judgment of God upon us may reinforce the persuasion of God; and, drawn by the ideal and hammered by the threat of punishment at the same time, we may find the way in which to build the structure of our common life.

It is the Christian faith that God forgives those who are honest with themselves about their sins, and who seek to turn from them. If God makes moral demands upon us and if failure to meet those demands gives us the sense of having fallen, that is not the end of the matter. If it were, the more sensitive we are the more we would be driven to complete despair or to self-deception. The revelation of God in Christ is a revelation of one who forgives those who repent. The evil in the past still has its consequences, but the individual is able to make a fresh start without being morally crippled by the burden of guilt.

There is much in the emphasis upon divine forgiveness in traditional forms of Christianity which quite rightly repels. Sometimes Christians have been too preoccupied with it; sometimes they have used it as a substitute for adequate moral effort; sometimes it has been narrowly conceived in relation to specific ecclesiastical practices and specific doctrines; sometimes it has been put into a framework of legalism, with the emphasis upon future rewards and punishments. But in our day we are again coming to see the importance of forgiveness. Modern psychiatry has revealed the degree to which the sense of guilt (even apart from its conventional religious manifestations), when it is unrelieved, can cripple a personality. Moreover, the social situation seems often to involve only possibilities which are in varying degrees evil, all of which give us a sense of having done wrong. Reinhold Niebuhr has come to emphasize the necessity of divine forgiveness in view of our entanglement in inescapable social evil. He says: "In every life there must at least be times and seasons when the good is felt as a present possession and not as a far-off goal,"* and he traces the possibility of that experience to the realization of the forgiveness of God.

If there were no such forgiveness, one of three things would be forced upon us: the denial of the binding character of moral obligations, the attempt to deceive ourselves about our achievements, or self-despair. To Christian faith this problem has always been an acute one and its promise of forgiveness to those who give up the attempt to deceive themselves and seek to *turn* from their sins is the word most needed at times in the experience of every honest soul.

It is the Christian faith that God can be trusted to deliver from frustration those who fulfil the conditions. The conditions are simple in the sense that they have nothing arbitrary or artificial about them, but they are not easy. They can be summed up in two words—commitment and trust. Men without the consciousness of God stumble on the fact that there is a

---

* *Reflections on the End of an Era*, p. 285.

healing power in life which goes beyond the obvious in delivering from frustration those who are not preoccupied with self. Worship is both the act of commitment and the exposure of our spirits to those things which can lift us and make us capable of commitment. There is here no stereotyped solution of all our human problems. There are puzzles to which we cannot see the answer, especially the puzzle that so many persons are so controlled by fear and self-concern that they cannot know the experience of healing when they need it most. But it is a matter of record that countless persons who have fulfilled the conditions have in the face of all the tragedies of life found deliverance for their spirits. It is one of the meanings of the cross that Jesus found such deliverance, though he experienced almost every form of external evil.

The confidence of Christians in personal immortality has been a way of underscoring this trust in God. It is the trust that not even death (which has all the appearance of being the final frustration for persons) is beyond the range of God's deliverance.

It is the Christian faith that there are evils in the world which God does not cause. Although most Christians would agree with that statement, they would differ in the range of its application and in the explanation of it. If we take seriously the belief that in man's freedom there is a source of evil by which the realization of God's purpose is limited, we can get real light on the most baffling problem which Christian faith faces—the problem of evil. A very large part of the evil in the world is the result of human action.

Some of it can be ascribed to ignorance; some of it to a conscious choice of evil or the lesser good. We must still ask the question: Why did not God create a world which would be fool-proof and knave-proof, in which the risks of human freedom could be avoided? The answer to that question is that God himself faces a limited number of possibilities. If he seeks to create a community of persons of tested moral worth, who are to be loyal sons and not puppets of the divine power, he can do so only on the basis of human freedom with all of its tragic cost. To have persons of developed intelligence it seems that he must also grant them freedom to learn by trial and error and to learn most by error when it hurts.

This is not a complete answer to the problem of evil—we still, for example, have unsolved the problem created by many forms of evil which are rooted in nature—but it does greatly reduce the problem. Evil which comes into the world through human agencies is not to be attributed to the intention of God. Nor is it to be attributed to a devil over against God. This kind of evil at least is the by-product of a structure of life which is the necessary condition for the highest good. In other words, evil is the result of freedom, and freedom is willed by God as the condition for the growth of persons. Along these lines it is possible for Christians to combine with their belief in God full realism concerning themselves and the world. They can thus avoid the greatest danger which besets religion—the danger of sanctifying the existing order of things because it is the creation of God.

It is the Christian faith that man combines in his nature high possibilities and tragic handicaps. One of the reasons for the adequacy of Christianity is that it is realistic about human nature. It avoids equally cynicism and sentimentalism. It sees the best in man and draws it out. Man is thought of as created in the image of God; and, though that image is distorted, glimpses of it are still present in human nature.

Wrapped up with man's freedom there is the fact of sin, and—as inevitable consequences of the limitations of his existence—there are failure and suffering. Man is not a finished creature living with a static character. As an individual and as a race, he is always at a particular point in a long process of growth—growth which is uneven and precarious. Moreover, man is limited in his knowledge, in the range of his imagination by the fact that he lives at a point in time and space, in a body, in a particular combination of social relationships. Even at his best, he never escapes the pull of inordinate self-interest, and this becomes a bias in favor of the group which is nearer, which is *his* group. In any particular situation it is impossible fully to untangle the strands which are the result of culpable selfishness, unavoidable ignorance, an external situation too complex and too much weighted with past evil to control. They are all there together creating man's problem. They will always be there to some degree so long as men are finite, but we cannot set definite limits to the degree to which men can rise above them. High possibilities—tragic handicaps: that is the Christian view of man.

It is the Christian faith that, in contrast to the habits of all history, there is a genuine equality of all men before God. This equality does not mean a dead level in ability, contribution, character, religious experience, but an equality in the fundamental right of all men to develop the possibilities within them. (More will be said about this idea of equality in Chapter III.)

The Christian idea of equality implies in our kind of world a substructure of economic justice and true equal opportunity in matters of bread and health and education and environment. Christian love is a mockery when content with anything less. Moreover, equality implies loyalty to a universal community according to which exclusive racialism and exclusive nationalism—the two distortions of life which are most tempting to our generation—are an offence against the God of all humanity.

It is the Christian faith that there is a movement of life in the world in which God is working most clearly to lift the level of the life of men. Christianity is not merely a set of ideas; it is primarily such a movement. This movement of life first appeared in the dim past when Hebrew religion emerged as something different from other Semitic cults, took clear form in the prophets of Israel, burst into the world with new clarity and power in Christ. It has continued its course, often cloudy and broken, in the Church; but it is not limited to the Church. To make the Church a more adequate vehicle for this movement of life is an absolute necessity for Christians in our day. As individuals, Christians are helpless in the face of the pagan forces in our world. They are thus being forced to rediscover in the Church an undergirding fellowship, a base for operations, and a collectivity which can stand up against the organized powers of the world.

.   .   .   .

In concluding this discussion of the meaning of Christianity in contrast to secularism I want to point out a fundamental divergence of Christianity from communism—the most self-conscious form of secularism.

It is the communists' belief that religion is the development of a pattern of "ideals" or fantasies as an escape from the frustrations of life. It is their belief further that, after the success of the revolution and after the complete eradication of the exploitation of capitalism, there will be no more frustration and hence there will be no more need for religion. Underlying that latter belief there is the assumption that evil is entirely the result of social conditions.

Christians find two fallacies in that communist attitude toward religion. The first is the assumption that religion is based solely upon frustration. For the Christian there are at least four other roots of religion. One is the opposite of frustration—joy and gratitude—a sense of the richness and beauty and goodness in the world and gratitude for life and all its gifts. A second root of religion is our response to moral demands which are made upon us in every social situation. Another root of religion is the discovery of the meaningfulness of existence through faith in God. It is not a question of weaving fantasies but of following the demands of rigorous thought in the interpretation of both man and nature. If God is, then to live as though he did not exist is to live in a world of illusion. A fourth root of religion for the Christian is discovery of the enhancement of life, the increase in the joy and depth and energy of living which goes with religious faith at its best.

The second fallacy of the communist interpretation of religion is the assumption that all human frustration comes from social conditions which a change in the economic system can remove. There are at least two other sources of frustration. One is the fact of sin and with it all the forms of human limitation which would to some degree create evil in any social order. The other is natural evil, and especially sickness and death. Religion is not merely the result of frustration, but it is true that frustration is one of the chief safeguards against complacency and against that human self-sufficiency which blinds us so easily to our real situation of dependence. And, no society, no matter how utopian it appears, will rob us of that.

In recognizing this inevitable human situation, Christianity is not only more realistic than communism; it also insures the existence within the society of the future of a standard, an ideal, which will judge that society as it judges our own. To believe that in any social order the ideal has been attained is to discourage growth. The growing point in the individual and in society is that tension between the ideal and actual attainment which Christianity provides and the need for which we can never outgrow.

CHAPTER II

THE CHRISTIAN ETHIC AND THE MORAL CONFUSION

For some time there has been great confusion over standards of personal morality. The morality of external religious authorities and the morality of convention or tabu have broken down. But, until the past few years, there did seem to be hope that, confused as we were about personal moral standards, the world was approaching a unified outlook in its social morality. During the decade of the twenties it did appear that democracy, internationalism, humanitarianism were becoming more and more widely accepted. The League of Nations embodied these ideals, and so did the democratic republics which had taken the place of the pre-war empires. But today the world is in greater confusion than ever in its social goals. It is the scene of a great conflict between democracy and dictatorship, between nationalism and internationalism, between racialism and universalism, between pacifism and militarism—not to speak of the conflicts between communism and capitalism or between communism and fascism, which cut across the other conflicts. Such confusion in morality leaves us without a sense of direction and is now more disastrous than any other single factor in our world.

Is there any secure moral truth which can be discovered? Are there any moral principles which are more solid than the conventions and tabus which have crashed around us?

This chapter is written out of the conviction that there is a moral structure in the world which can be discovered, and that this structure can be known apart from any religious authority. Nevertheless, as was suggested in the last chapter, the ultimate question, "Why is the good binding on me?" leads us to the threshold of religion. There is an order of consequences in life which neither individuals nor social groups can long defy without bringing obvious punishment upon themselves. This morality, based upon our general human experience, is not in itself the whole Christian ethic but it is the substructure on which that ethic is based. I shall first sketch briefly some of the elements in this common morality which are necessary if our human life is to hold together, and then I shall suggest how that morality is crowned by the specifically Christian ethic.

In setting forth the content of this common morality, I shall mention four general moral principles which are rooted in the structure of life.

1. *Beyond Individualistic Egoism*

Individualistic egoism is seldom held up as a moral ideal to be espoused, though the conduct of all of us is streaked with it. Now it is true that there is no inevitable spectacular punishment which overtakes the egoist. If he is a man of violence, he may meet his fate at the hands of other men of violence. If underneath he is a person of some sensitivity, he may find himself tortured by fear and by the sense of the very narrowness which goes with preoccupation with self. But it is not impossible that there is such a thing as a cool, calculating egoist who, for example, may poison the mind of a generation with his newspapers, and die in old age amidst his flatterers, an apparent success. But it would be well to ask several questions about such an apparently successful egoist.

What has he missed? Does he not really cover up more frustration than he admits to himself? He has forfeited the possibility of living a life of devotion to anything beyond himself—more meaningful and more permanent than himself. He has forfeited the natural confidence of his contemporaries; he is feared rather than respected or trusted or loved.

What would the world be like if his way of life became general?

Must even he not keep his self-respect by means of self-deception?

Does he really admire in others the kind of person he is himself?

Would he truly desire to have his children cut according to his pattern?

How long does it take to see through him after his death? It is then no longer to any one's interest to flatter. In these days there is a relentlessness about history in showing up the hollowness of selfish men of power. The technique of Congressional investigation has speeded up the process of historical judgment, and men find themselves exposed in all their emptiness while they are still alive.

I think the foregoing questions suggest how true it is that our common rejection of individualistic egoism as an ideal is no mere convention but is rooted in stubborn facts in personal and social life.

2. *Beyond Group Egoism to Universalism*

But individualistic egoism as an accepted ideal is not our greatest danger. Far more powerful in our world, because it is widely accepted as an ideal, is the egoism of social groups. We have the spectacle of groups drawing circles around themselves and affirming that outside of those circles they have no obligation. This is true of national groups, of racial groups, and to some extent of class groups. I say of class groups "to some extent" because there is a profound difference at this point between the class consciousness of communism and other radical movements and the nationalism of fascism. Communism seeks a universal society in which there will be no exploitation by any group. It intends its class consciousness to be only temporary until the privilege and power of the ruling class are destroyed, and it expects that in the new society there will be no classes. The class consciousness of privileged groups (which is in America at the present time more pronounced than the class consciousness of the workers) is never admitted to be class consciousness at all; it always claims to be struggle for a universal good, such as Liberty, or Americanism, or the Constitution. It is in nationalism and racialism as ideals, recognized as such with no sense of their temporary and provisional character, that we see the clearest examples of group egoism.

There are at least two factors in the structure of life which make nationalism and racialism evil. In the first place, such racialism and nationalism exaggerate human differences and fly in the face of a real human kinship deeper than all differences. It is hardly necessary to argue with scientific evidence against the doctrine of racial purity and superiority with which racialism is rationalized. More important than such arguments is the fact that we need to have only one friend within another race or nation to see how absurd such racial doctrines are. One such friend who is understood and loved is a kind of hostage for the conviction that there is a universal humanity which underlies differences. Not all the shrieking of a Goebbels or a Streicher can prevent individual Germans from discovering the common humanity of individual Jews. Moreover, there is a recognition of this general human kinship in our attitude toward suffering in those of another group. Our ready appreciation of children of all groups is perhaps a guarantee of a common humanity; it is more than our appreciation of kittens when we are intolerant of cats. Any theory or way of life which fails to recognize the real unity of humanity is palpably false, and our experience will break through it.

The second reason for believing that group egoism goes against the grain of the world is now too obvious for our comfort. A world organized on the principle of group egoism is headed straight for war. The exponents of group egoism at times glorify war. Two European statesmen recently declared that the battle-field is to men what motherhood is to women, and that therefore it is both natural and noble. A British paper characterized such sentiments as "bloody nonsense," and that is all that needs to be said. Any nobility war may acquire from the fact that men sacrifice themselves is lost in the fact that they only sacrifice themselves incidentally to killing. But argument is unfortunately not needed, for the fact is too plain that war in the long run means vast collective suicide: that is refutation enough of any ideal. The consequences of group egoism are not limited to war. In an interdependent world they lead to economic strangulation, from which all suffer. The need of general sanitation suggests the same thing, because germs respect neither boundaries nor races; they will cross the railroad tracks and attack "the better element." To plan only for the welfare of one group, to stir up one group against another, to recognize no obligation outside of one's group is to bring punishment upon all groups. This fact (which it is fortunately trite to mention) makes nonsense of the ideal which is set forth by the articulate leadership of great nations.

3. *Personal Discipline*

A third principle of which we can be certain is that in our personal lives the "better things" cannot be experienced without personal discipline. That gives us real guidance if all that we mean by the "better things" is those things which give lasting satisfaction, those which grow, those which can be shared, those which lead to richer and expanding life. A personal life which is undisciplined, at loose ends, leads inevitably into blind alleys. A life preoccupied with drink or sex or gambling cannot fail to have this result. There is this much solid ground under some of our older conventional morality.

One interesting confirmation of this position can be seen in the experience of the Soviet Union. Russian communists have no interest in American bourgeois morality. They would reject it out of hand because it is ours. And yet they in their own way, out of their own experience, have stumbled upon some of the same moral ideas which have been a part of our bourgeois morality. For example, they have discovered that they cannot have a successful society in a complicated technical age except on the basis of temperance. Drunken workmen and engineers would defeat any Plan. For this reason the communists have developed methods of temperance education which could teach something to our professional advocates of temperance. Members of the Communist Party are held up to a standard of strict personal discipline at all points where their effectiveness is threatened.

Increasingly in the matter of sex ethics, Russian Communism is coming to emphasize the importance of the family. Divorce has been made more difficult. War has been made on prostitution, which is regarded as an inheritance from capitalism. Sidney and Beatrice Webb in their authoritative study of the trends in the Soviet Union sum up what seems to be the present emphasis within the Communist Party:

"Stability and mutual loyalty [in marriage] have become steadily more generally enforced not only by public opinion but also, so far as Party members and Comsomols [young communists] were concerned, by the ordinary Party sanctions. Disloyalty in marital relations, and even exceptional instability have become definite offences against communist ethics, leading not only to reprimands, but also, in bad cases, to expulsion."*

I cite this Russian experience because it illustrates so perfectly the contention that sound morality is not a matter of tabu or arbitrary authority but is based upon a structure of things which men will discover no matter from where they start. This is just as true in matters of personal discipline as in the morality of social groups. Our task is to disentangle that which is solid and sure in our more conventional moral principles from the petty forms of legalism which have come to cling to them; for the latter always bring discredit upon the former and lead to the kind of moral confusion from which we are suffering.

4. *Integrity*

There is nothing more necessary in our kind of world than that we be able to trust each other, that there be real correspondence between what we say and what we think, between what we say and what we do. It is even difficult for us to live with ourselves if we are conscious of a lie in our souls. A part of the protest against conventional morals arises out of this very hatred of shams which is one of the sound

* *Soviet Communism: A New Civilization?* Vol. II, p. 1057.

things in contemporary life. This however is being undermined by the policy of manufacturing shams by means of propaganda which is thought to be in the interest of the group.

There are those who write as though our emphasis upon integrity, common honesty, were a by-product of our capitalist civilization. But, although it is true that the relationships of credit and exchange in capitalism make honesty necessary (though capitalism in other ways puts a strain upon honesty), any complicated economic system in the modern world with its exchange of goods at a distance would require the same honesty.

Science, one of the permanent interests of humanity, could not progress without integrity. It is dependent upon the fact that scientists can be trusted to report what they find and not what they would like to find.

Ordinary communication would be impossible without integrity. One illustration of this fact can be drawn from what seems to be an exception to the general rule of integrity. There may be times when it is right to deceive, to tell "white lies." Such an occasion would be the protection of a friend against the secret police of one of our contemporary dictators. But here is the rub. People do not succeed in deceiving unless they have the reputation for telling the truth, and if they deceive too often their deceptions are self-defeating. This suggests that even the apparent exception of "white lies" confirms the general principle of integrity.

So far I have suggested that there are at least four moral principles which are so rooted in the structure of life that we cannot avoid discovering them in the long run. To fill out the picture, I shall take up two important institutions which are a matter of controversy—democracy and monogamy. Are they matters of convention or do they have a more solid basis in life?

Democracy

When I speak of democracy I do not refer to a particular set of parliamentary institutions which may or may not be adapted to the complexities of a modern state. It is a mistake to prejudge the degree to which the administration of government should be delegated to experts. But there are two elements in democracy which are more fundamental than any such machinery, and which may be considered to be permanently valid. One is the principle that in the long run, government should rest upon the consent of the governed. The other is that there should be freedom of expression for minority groups. Without such freedom the principle of "consent" is valueless, because it is possible for those who have power to regiment opinion in their own interests and to prevent any real exercise of choice on the part of the governed. The Hitler plebiscites seem to the outside world to be examples of this latter tendency to the point of caricature.

These two elements in democracy are demanded by the structure of life for at least four reasons. (1) Without them there can be no final protection against the abuse of power. Irresponsible power is sure to be used in the interests of the group which possesses it. This is not merely the result of ordinary selfishness which is under too great temptation. It is also the result of the fact that such a ruling group is inevitably cut off from the people who fear it; it becomes unable to see the world from their point of view. (2) Only where there is freedom of expression is it possible for the truth to work on the minds of men. The final argument against all forms of repression is that they make truth subservient to the interests of the powerful and cut off that experiment with ideas on which the discovery of new truth depends. (3) Democratic government, even when it is most inefficient, is an educational process by which persons learn how to exercise responsibility. (4) Without these two elements in democracy there is no way in which to provide for orderly change. No opposition party is developed which can take over power without social convulsions; the only recourse when power is abused is revolt. We can see in the world today what a vicious circle men are caught in when they discard democracy. That circle consists of dictatorship—abused power—revolt— dictatorship—abused power—revolt. As a result of this vicious circle, and of the wars with which dictators divert the people, a shadow is cast on the future until the world finds its way back to responsible government and freedom.

Monogamy

The other controversial institution which is to be considered is monogamy. I want to suggest four reasons why monogamy stands out clearly as the ideal form of relationship between the sexes. The fact that monogamy is the ideal does not settle all questions of sex ethics: for example, questions concerning relations before marriage, concerning what is right when marriage is impossible or when a particular marriage has failed. But, it does give us a fixed point from which to get light on these questions.

1. Monogamy is the only institution which seems to do justice to the interests of women, to respect them fully as persons, to provide them with security. It is partly because of this that the communists have found it necessary to make divorce more difficult. It is a plain fact of history that under conditions of monogamy the level of the life of women has been raised far higher than in civilizations in which other forms of relationship are the standard.

2. Monogamous marriage provides the most favorable environment for the development of children. With all the dangers of possessiveness in parental affection, children need the emotional security provided by the monogamous home.

3. Monogamy integrates the sex side of life most effectively with the whole of life. Nothing could be more distracting than to have life one love affair after another. The stability which marriage gives enables us to get on with the job.

4. When marriage is successful, or when we see examples of its success, we do not need argument to convince us that we want nothing other than monogamy. Nothing else seems to promise such enduring joy, such

an opportunity for comradeship, growing affection, discipline, and emotional security.

Lenin's position in regard to marriage was once summarized by one of his followers in these words: "We would not mix in a man's affairs if he changed his wife every third day, *if his children and his work did not suffer from that.*"* That sentence says only half of what needs to be said, but it does say that half effectively. No form of relationship between the sexes can be the right one unless it meets at least those tests. If we add to them full respect for the personalities of all concerned and the conditions for the highest and most enduring satisfaction, we would not be far from a basis upon which an ethic for sex relationships could rest more solidly than it has rested in the past. It is because monogamy fits into the inevitable demands of life that we can accept the Christian teaching that it is ordained of God.

The Christian Ethic

There are those who believe that they do honor to the Christian ideal to treat it as though it were wholly separate from the morality which can be hammered out in our common experience. But, it is the greatness of Christianity that it fits the facts of life, facts which can be discerned by those who do not claim to be Christians. In what has been said we have a kind of substructure of morality without which our life cannot in the long run be held together. If that were

---

* *Op. cit.*, p. 1057. *See* on pp. 1054-1056 an account of Lenin's interview on sex morality with Clara Zetkin.

not in line with the Christian ideal, one would be quite justified in questioning the truth of that ideal. Moreover, in a world in which Christians and non-Christians must live together it is essential to have a common morality the truth of which all can see.

The recognition of the falseness of individualistic egoism, the necessity of universalism, of personal discipline, of integrity, together with such institutions as democracy and monogamy, form such a foundation for the Christian ideal. It is true that in the past Christianity has more often than not been associated with autocratic and oligarchic societies; but democracy, where its success is possible, is more favorable for the Christian life. Those Christian theorists who still toy with the idea that a government by those who govern in virtue of some divine right will preserve Christian ideals more surely than a government which is responsive to the people fail to reckon with the fact that power is too tempting to those who wield it. In practice, such a government (which, because it claims to be rooted in a higher commission, does not hold itself responsible to the "common horde") will find itself standing for something less than the justice which the "common horde" can understand and without which a society is corrupted, no matter what graces may be developed among a few.

In the Middle Ages Christian thinkers thought in terms of two sets of virtues: the cardinal virtues, such as wisdom and temperance and justice and courage; and the Christian graces: faith, hope, and love. The first set of virtues Christians shared with pagan idealists. It is some such scheme as that which I am suggesting. Here we have the cardinal virtues without which life cannot be held together—"beyond-egoism," universalism, discipline, integrity. Above them but dependent upon them are certain Christian graces. These are the flowering of the Christian life.

What are these Christian graces? I suggest three. The first of them is humility. That is not a good word, but it means the absence of self-righteousness and self-importance. It means having an objective view of oneself. It means seeing oneself in all one's dependence for existence and achievement and welfare upon God. The second is sensitiveness—sensitiveness, which goes beyond the obvious, to the needs and feelings of others. The third is commitment—the commitment of self which will go the second and third mile, which will swear to its own hurt and change not; which will pay the price of the cross. What we mean by Christian love is not any one thing. It involves all these graces, especially the last two; and it grows out of that unselfishness and that universalism which belong to the substructure of the Christian life.

How do we know that these Christian graces are good? I doubt if we can prove that they are necessary to hold life together, although it is true that, if integrity is carried very far in our kind of world, it will involve the cost of commitment. We can know that these graces are good because when we see them embodied in the lives of others we admire them, and because they make possible for ourselves a higher fulfilment of life. The reckoning up of the consequences of our conduct can carry us far in ethics. Merely the avoiding of blind alleys can give us real moral guidance. But in the end our ethical life must depend on what we appreciate as the good when we see it embodied in persons.

CHAPTER III

CHRISTIANITY AND THE ECONOMIC ORDER

Our present economic order grew up when the Church was asleep. As Professor Tawney has shown, the economic and political orders became lost provinces so far as the Church was concerned in the centuries between the Protestant Reformation and the very recent past. Just within the past half-century the churches have begun to recognize that Christianity has a responsibility for the economic life of the world. Perhaps, even if the churches had been fully awake concerning economic developments during the rise of capitalism, they would have been unable to keep up with events. What we must underline is the fact that this economic system which so largely controls our lives grew up with an amazing rapidity in response to the developments of modern technology, in response to the almost breathless opening up of new territories for exploitation especially in our own West, and in response to the thrust for profit on the part of countless individuals—some of them "robber barons" but most of them men who lived within the moral code of their generation. No one planned this system. It grew up as a result of the converging of these forces with very little restraint or guidance from moral or religious ideals. In fact, the more recent developments of capitalism have not been restrained even by classical economic theory with its emphasis upon free trade and competition. But here it is—this system which is the dominant social force in our world, which conditions the welfare, security, and vocational choices of the people, and (more than they know) molds their character and ideals.

This economic system is characterized by the ownership of the means of production by private individuals and corporations and is for the most part avowedly run for the sake of the profit of the owners. It is assumed by its defenders that the by-product of this activity for the sake of profit will be the public welfare in the form of the maximum production and the widespread distribution of wealth through wages.

Capitalism is criticized from two points of view. There are those who say that it is unable any longer to function without increasingly serious break-downs, and that its tendency now is to curtail total production; that it has reached the stage in which its expansion through the discovery of new markets is no longer rapid enough to absorb the goods which are produced; and that it is incapable of providing a market among its own workers because of the tendency to preserve profits at the expense of lower prices and higher wages. This line of criticism is very widely accepted, and I have yet to hear it convincingly refuted. But in so far as it rests upon strictly economic issues there is room for Christians to differ. In this book we are not concerned with this type of criticism.

There is, however, another kind of criticism which

calls attention to the effect which capitalism has upon persons. In regard to this moral criticism of capitalism it is difficult to see how Christians who face the facts can continue to differ. I shall now call attention to three points at which there is a conflict between Christianity and capitalism as it has been developed in America.

1. There is first of all the staggering degree of inequality which capitalism permits. It is no exaggeration to say that, in spite of our democratic forms, our country is run for the benefit of the top third of its citizens and that the bottom third are definitely the victims of the economic process. The Brookings Institute report, which is based upon assumptions favorable to the continuance of capitalism, has made very vivid the degree of this inequality. In days of apparent prosperity, in 1929, it shows, 36,000 families had an aggregate income equal to the aggregate income of 11,600,000 families. Or put in another way, one-tenth of 1 per cent of the population had an income equal to that of 41 per cent of the population. Even in normal times large sections of the American people are excluded from the feast of American prosperity. That is true for example of the Negroes, of unorganized unskilled workers, of tenant farmers. In times of depression the number of those who are excluded is very much larger; and the exclusion means for them unemployment, complete insecurity, with hunger never far away.

This inequality is serious for what it means in poverty and lack of opportunity for masses of men, women and children. It denies them decent housing; it deprives them of needed medical care; it means too little leisure or too much idleness; it limits the opportunity for education; it creates fear for the future which is quite unnecessary in our society; it means that millions of young people can grow up without ever having consecutive work.

This inequality is also serious because it encourages the more privileged section of society to live in waste and luxury with an utterly false sense of values and also to live in the most callous disregard of what their superior privilege means to the victims of the economic process. To have society run so largely for your benefit, to be callous to the fact that millions lack what you take for granted as necessities, to assume as a result of greater privilege an attitude of self-importance and superiority to the very people who are your victims (thus literally adding insult to injury) is fatal to the Christian life. The result of this whole situation is that fellowship becomes extremely difficult. We have castes separated by snobbishness and bitterness.

2. Capitalism puts a premium on selfishness and deception. The very defense which is given for capitalism is that it insures effective activity by appealing to the acquisitive side of human nature. Even if it were possible to iron out many of the inequalities which it has produced and to return to a purely competitive type of capitalism which would prevent the large concentrations of wealth and power, it would still have this difficulty for Christians. It must be admitted that in any society ways will have to be found

to enlist the self-regarding motives on the side of efficiency. In that sense we cannot expect to outgrow the profit motive completely. But the evil in capitalism is that it exercises and develops that motive far too much, and does not seek to develop other motives. The more constructive side of human nature—the desire to do a good job or loyalty to the community and its needs—tends to atrophy; and the most powerful motive of all (which can be either constructive or destructive)—the desire for social approval—is turned into channels of acquisitiveness by a society which honors wealth as the chief symbol of success.

Selfishness is easily carried to the point of complete callousness or to the willingness to deceive. We become callous to the exploitation which is incidental to our comfort (especially if it is at a distance). We become callous to the use which is made of what we produce, especially when we produce the munitions of war or the raw materials which go into the munitions of war. Also, a premium is put on deception. How large a part of salesmanship involves deception? It may be subtle insinuations or it may be exaggerations which are intended to deceive more often than obvious lies. It is only necessary to ask that question.

3. Under the form of capitalism which has developed in America, there is a vast and increasing concentration of economic power. This is the result of the growth of corporations and the control of corporations by even more gigantic financial institutions. It is partly the result of the common class interests which bind together in their relation to labor even those who

are competitors.   The organs of public opinion—the newspapers most obviously, but also to some degree our educational institutions and churches—are controlled by a climate created by the class interest of those who have most economic power.   One result of this concentration of economic power is that it tends to undermine political democracy without destroying its forms.   I do not want to exaggerate this, and to speak as many do of our "bogus democracy," for we still have health in our democracy (especially when it is compared with fascism); and yet this tendency to undermine democracy is always a powerful factor in our society.

This concentration of power has one effect to which I want to give emphasis.   It makes most people afraid. They are afraid to lose their jobs if they have them; they are afraid to lose relief if they are unemployed; teachers are afraid to speak their convictions; ministers are afraid to antagonize sources of the churches' income; workers are afraid to speak their minds or to let it be known how they vote; and many of the rest of us are afraid to antagonize the powers that be in the community for fear of losing customers or clients.   This fear is a terrible threat to personal integrity because it makes conformity so much safer than action in line with convictions.

At the present, the only way to overcome this fear is to organize those who are afraid.   They must be organized into labor unions, teachers' unions, farm tenant unions, coöperatives, and in other ways.   This organization of those who are afraid, if it is successful, inevitably leads to social struggle and bitterness. This stage of bitterness is more wholesome and constructive than the stage of fear. Both create serious obstacles to the Christian life. What I want to stress is that under capitalism with its concentration of irresponsible economic power it must be one or the other—*fear* or *bitterness*.

Under our present economic system the Christian is forced to lead a double life. He cannot live at all without living off the exploitation of workers and the deception of consumers, and under present conditions he lives off the productions of the munitions of war or the materials necessary for the munitions of war. The immediate sources of one's income may be innocent enough, but we have only to ask about the sources of the incomes of the people who pay the people who pay the people who pay us. Moreover, it is leading a double life to express high sentiments about Christian love and yet to live in our relative privilege side by side with desperate human need. Without a change in our economic order on a large scale there is no escape from this double life, for the best efforts of the individual Christian cannot get beyond rather ineffectual asceticism or philanthropy. To work for structural change, for a world in which such compromises will be unnecessary, is the only way for the Christian to preserve his integrity.

THE CHRISTIAN MESSAGE FOR THE ECONOMIC ORDER

Christianity is not an economic program. It is not, as we are sometimes told, "an alternative to communism." But it is an interpretation of life with which certain economic programs, including capitalism as we know it, are in contradiction, and by which all economic programs must be tested. An economic order based upon the social ownership of the large sources of wealth and power would probably be far more favorable than capitalism for the Christian life. But the precise form that such an order should take and the methods of bringing it about cannot be deduced from Christianity. Moreover, we must not forget that there would be great dangers to spiritual freedom in a more collectivistic society; but to use that danger as an excuse for preserving the *status quo,* which in fact regiments the conditions of life of the masses while preserving the economic freedom of owners and employers and entrepreneurs, is the worst kind of moral confusion. It is theoretically possible that a decentralized economic system in which monopolies are really broken up and in which the results of the new technology are passed on to the people through lower prices—the kind of system which the Brookings Institute or Senator Borah would approve—would be on the whole as satisfactory as any; but even that would overstimulate the acquisitiveness of men. One would have to weigh the danger from that acquisitiveness over against the dangers to individual freedom in collectivism. The question is whether or not such a decentralized economic order is within the bounds of possibility in America in its present state of development. Although one may have strong opinions on that point, again, the answer to the question cannot be deduced from Christianity. This discussion, in spite of its brevity, should be enough to illustrate the general position that Christianity is in contradiction with some forms of economic life but that it does not imply any particular economic system.

The most important contribution of Christianity to this discussion is that it involves a form of human equality. The word "equality" may easily be misunderstood. Men are obviously not equal in physique, ability, character, contribution, religious experience. From the Christian point of view, men are equal only in the right before God to develop the best possibilities in their personalities. But that means that the denial of that kind of opportunity to the masses of men in our society is not only immoral; it is also blasphemous. It would be well to contemplate how it must appear in the sight of God for a small section of humanity to strut with self-importance on top of the rest, denying to others the opportunity which they claim for themselves. This situation is not relieved but only made the more hypocritical when comfortable Christians tell themselves that, since material things are unimportant, such matters as the distribution of wealth are irrelevant to their concern as Christians. This rests on the assumption that the soul can develop its highest possibilities regardless of external circumstances. What is forgotten is that although that is relatively true of persons in the high stages of spiritual development, it is not true of children and average men and women. For them denial of equal opportunity on the economic level is often equivalent to the denial of equal opportunity on the spiritual level. Christian love becomes a mockery if it rests content with anything less than equal opportunity on both levels for all.

There is one difficulty which keeps Christians from seeing the economic implications of the gospel in our time. In the New Testament it is taken for granted that poverty is inevitable. In the time of Jesus the world appeared to be a static world, or at least one in which social change could not be effected by the organized effort of the followers of Jesus. Moreover, it was doubtless true that poverty was inevitable: "The poor ye shall have always with you." In that situation the best that was possible for the followers of Jesus was philanthropy, or the realization of true fellowship within the Christian community. Christian love took the form inevitably of giving to relieve need. It is of the utmost importance to realize that we now live in a society in which poverty is not necessary—in which it is possible to raise the economic level of the whole population to a point at which there will be a decent standard of life and genuine equal opportunity for all. (Authoritative estimates of the standard of living which is technologically possible in America range from $2,000 to $5,000 per year per family. Either estimate would involve the end of poverty.) That means that philanthropy in the conventional sense would become irrelevant, and in its place the relevant implementation of Christian love would be a just distribution of wealth. It is the task of this generation of Christians to translate the idea of love in its relation to the economic problem from terms of philanthropy into terms of justice.

One further contribution of Christianity to a solution of the economic problem is that Christianity is oriented toward common human need. This fact is lost sight of by those who over-spiritualize their ideas of life. It has been said that "Christianity is the most materialistic religion in the world," and that is probably true. Jesus emphasized in his activity of healing the importance of the body. He announced at the inauguration of his ministry that he came to relieve humanity at the point of common need; that he came "to preach good tidings to the poor, to proclaim release to the captives, and recovering of sight to the blind, to set at liberty them that are bruised." In the story of the Last Judgment he separated the sheep from the goats on the basis of their attitude to everyday human need—economic need.

At the heart of the Lord's Prayer there is a petition which guarantees the "materialism" of Christianity: "Give us this day our daily bread." That petition has become meaningless to those whose daily bread is assured. It would gain new meaning which would be true to its original spirit if we allowed a commentary to run through our minds as we pray that prayer. It would run in this way: "Give us this day the brains and the conscience so to organize our economic life that the bread which thou hast already given us in abundance may not rot but may be distributed to meet the needs of all people."

A final contribution of Christianity to the economic

problem, harder for us to assimilate, is the fact that
Jesus so clearly condemned wealth. Try to tone his
sayings down as we will, there can be no escape from
Jesus' profound distrust of wealth. "It is easier for a
camel to go through a needle's eye than for a rich man
to enter into the kingdom of God." Dives was not condemned as an exploiter of Lazarus—as one who had any
special responsibility for Lazarus. It was enough that
he lived in the same world with Lazarus, callously en-
joying his privilege. This distrust of wealth is no
aberration to be explained away, but an evidence of
the wisdom of Jesus. Wealth does distract the soul
with things. It does create an artificial sense of self-
importance which injures both religious humility and
right relations with others. It creates a barrier to
fellowship. It causes one to have a stake in the *status
quo* which blinds one to the need of change and makes
one's mind a nest of rationalizations in the defence
of one's own privilege.

This distrust of wealth which Christianity teaches
suggests that, although there is a conflict between Christianity and our capitalistic order because of the unjust
poverty which the latter permits, there will also be a
serious tension between Christianity and any economic
order in which there is such abundance that every
class can have a luxurious standard of life. That will
be something to watch when the time comes. In the
meantime, there are two things to be said. Although
abundance does have its own dangers, if there is justice
in its distribution, it is no bar to fellowship. And
Christian thinkers should be slow in criticizing any

future situation which would mean that the under-privileged would then have no more than they themselves have had so long that they have come to take it for granted.

It is necessary to define the relation between the contribution of Christianity to the struggle for economic justice and the other factors in that struggle. The Christian must first of all realize that social change will not come merely because people are controlled by Christian ideals. Change comes when old systems disintegrate because of the contradictions within them. Change comes from the organized pressure of those who are the victims of the existing social order. This organized pressure from the victims of society is morally mixed, for they are driven by economic interest, jealousy, hatred, a high solidarity, a passion for justice, a realistic understanding of the order of things from which they suffer. As Reinhold Niebuhr has said: "The executors of judgment in history are always driven by both hunger and dreams, by both the passions of warfare and the hope of the city of God."*

If the Christian is not to be an ineffectual spectator concerned more about the purity of his own soul than about results in society, he must coöperate with those political and social movements which at a given time seem most promising in the light of Christian ideals. The program of the future cannot be imposed on society by theorists; it will be hammered out in the give and take of the political struggle itself. By entering that struggle from the Christian motive one can have

* Reflections on the End of an Era, p. 140.

a part in the raising of the moral level of the whole struggle and in the fashioning of the program. To take part in any political struggle is to compromise. The very mixture of motives which has been mentioned means that every political movement or program is corrupted to some degree. The nearer such a movement is to success the more it attracts to its ranks those who see in it a road to power. But to remain aloof from such movements is to acquiesce in the *status quo,* and that is a more serious compromise for the Christian.

I shall conclude this discussion of Christianity and the economic order with a few words about the specific place of the Church as a Church in the struggle for economic justice. The Christian as a citizen cannot escape the obligation to take some part directly in the social movements which, with all the mixture of motives behind them, point in the most hopeful direction; but the Church as a Church should not allow itself to become too closely identified with any political movement or program. It has however three contributions to make which are of great importance.

1. In the first place, as Dr. F. Ernest Johnson has said, the main task of the Church is an inside job;** it must bring its own members to a new attitude. It must help its own members to see what Christianity demands of society. Through the failure of the Church's teaching in the past, most of its members are unaware that such demands exist; they regard Christianity as little more than sanctification of what their

** *The Church and Society, passim.*

own class calls respectable. It must help its own members to see the realities in the existing social situation, and especially to see themselves as they are in relation to that situation. For the most part the Protestant churches are at present best able to reach the middle classes; but in America the middle classes have the balance of power. Without a large measure of coöperation (or at least acquiescence) from those classes no drastic social change is possible except at the cost of civil war. If our churches brought a large number of their members to the point where they could see through the rationalizations with which they defend their privilege, where they could realize the degree to which their opinions, their social philosophies, their political loyalties are molded by a narrow class interest; and where they may acquire the habit of putting the burden of proof on all opinions which coincide with their own interest—if our churches seriously attempted these things, they would go far to prepare the way for peaceful social change. So far these things have not been tried on a large scale.

2. In the second place, the Church may well stand for a few definite social objectives. These should be chosen with great discrimination, but there are at least two such objectives which must underlie any possible program which can be realized without civil war and dictatorship. One of these is freedom of expression for minority groups. The other is freedom of economic groups to organize for their own protection. To defend the rights of the less powerful groups to organize into independent labor unions or into coöperatives is

to have a part at the very point where the issue will be joined in the immediate future. This is not to espouse a particular program but rather to promote the conditions which are essential for the peaceful development of any program.

3. The churches should teach their members concerning the importance of taking part in the most promising social and economic movements. Without dictating as to what movements they should join, it should teach the importance of political action, and at the same time show realistically the dangers of compromise in all such action, in order that Christians may not give themselves to any political movement with blind allegiance.

When a new order comes, the Church must not become so closely entangled with that order as it has been entangled with the present one. It should be there to keep the new order under criticism, and to help to preserve it from the corruptions which have almost destroyed the old.

CHAPTER IV

CHRISTIANITY AND THE NEW TYRANNY

Since the war, Christians have found themselves, almost without warning, confronted by a new type of tyranny: the tyranny of the totalitarian state—the state which claims the whole of life. The fascist dictatorships have been the most conspicuous examples of this state tyranny but the general tendency to magnify the state is very wide-spread. This tyranny is accompanied by a resurgence of violent nationalism. In Germany in particular, nationalism is reinforced by an even more fanatical emphasis upon race. Along with tyranny and nationalism go the militarization of large populations and the threat of another world war.

There is nothing new about tyranny, but the modern tyrant has the advantage over his predecessors in that he has all the resources provided by modern science. He can more completely regiment a population than was ever before possible. He has at his command the radio, with which he can poison millions of minds overnight. He has all the techniques of modern education with which to mold the minds and souls of the rising generation. The airplane has destroyed distance, and has made him almost omnipresent in his own dominions. He has the modern weapons of warfare at his back which make it extremely difficult to carry on a successful revolt. Moreover, he makes a point of appealing to no higher law

49

than his own will or the will of the party or nation which he represents. Since the rise of Christianity, it has been the custom for tyrants to recognize a will above their own even if they have done it only lip service. But as a result of the secularization of life which was discussed in the first chapter, even what restraint there was in that recognition of a higher law has disappeared. What could be more terrifying than the power, both political and technical, which has been put into the hands of men who acknowledge no standards above the will of the state which they rule or the party which they represent? Freedom is destroyed, objective truth has given place to lies in the interests of state policy, cruelty toward persons and especially toward the most courageous and independent persons has been revived, the peace machinery which seemed to be the one gain from the last war has been sabotaged, and, finally, never very far away is the threat of world catastrophe.

One feature of this new tyranny which should be emphasized is very well presented by Christopher Dawson in his book, *Religion and the Modern State.* He points out the degree to which the modern state (and this is true to some degree even of democratic states) has taken on responsibility for the souls of its citizens. It takes a whole generation and molds its attitude toward life through its systems of education and propaganda. Where the state has an official philosophy, as in the Soviet Union and in the fascist countries, it makes that philosophy do the work of religious beliefs and moral convictions among the generation which it has been able to mold in this way. As Dawson says: "If the new State threatens the freedom of the Church and the individual conscience, it is because it is itself taking on some of the features of a church and is no longer content to confine itself to the outside of life—the sphere of the policeman and the lawyer. It claims the whole of life and thus becomes a competitor of the Church on its own ground."*

Up to this point in the discussion conditions in other countries have been emphasized as though the United States were free from the kind of menace which has been described. It is important that we neither assume that our country will follow European patterns nor regard our situation with self-righteous complacency.

There were factors in the European situation which are not operative here. The humiliations of the war and the peace fed the Hitler movement. A similar feeling of national inferiority has been an important factor in the development of Italian nationalism. Moreover, it is still true that no country which has had a long and relatively successful experiment with democracy has abandoned it for dictatorship. Also, the economic stringency which makes the middle classes ripe for fascist demagogues is more inescapable as the world is now organized in Germany and Italy than in the United States. Perhaps, most important is the fact that on this continent the heritage of conflict is absent; although our unarmed northern boundary is not a sign of superior virtue but of great historical good fortune.

---

* p. 44.

In spite of these real advantages we have in America several dangers which must be noted.

1. We have at hand the materials out of which an exclusive nationalism might well develop. Our provincialism, our habit of self-righteousness toward the rest of the world, the fact that as a nation we are quickly swayed by mass emotion, our susceptibility to demagoguery which has a strong nationalist bias, the failure of the great majority of Americans who believe in peace to oppose tendencies toward militarism, the official doctrine promulgated by the Supreme Court that the state is the final authority over the conscience—these are only the most important factors which might well arouse in us a dangerous form of nationalism.

2. There is at present a rapid intensification of the social struggle in America. The passing of the frontier, the contraction of foreign markets, the promise of an abundance which is withheld, the long period of depression accompanied by a deep foreboding that unemployment has become a permanent problem, the violence against labor and the attacks on civil liberties, the rise of all kinds of movements controlled by class interests as diverse as the industrial union movement, the Townsend Movement, and the American Liberty League, the strong passions aroused by the 1936 election—these are hints of the intensification of the social struggle which at least suggests European developments. In such a situation there is a great danger that democracy will be sacrificed, though the danger is far greater from those who fear that the votes of masses will be used to undermine their privilege

than from those who would sacrifice democracy to the purposes of revolution.

3. The possibility of two events should be put beside the tendencies which have been mentioned. If America should find herself once more in a state of deep economic depression or if she should become involved in war, only a miracle could save us from the social convulsions out of which some form of fascism would probably emerge. Such a period of depression would complete the despair of large sections of the American people and make them willing to follow any leader who promised them a specious deliverance. A war would furnish an excuse for all forms of repression.

These suggestions about the possible developments in America are not written in order to provide the material for facile prophecies but merely to show that the problems for Christians which are created by the developments in Europe are not merely academic for Americans. To some degree and in some form they may become our problems. At present it is the task of American Christians to deal constructively with the situations out of which the chief dangers arise.

Now we shall turn to the contribution of the Christian religion in the face of this whole trend toward tyranny, nationalism, and war.

1. *Christianity keeps alive the emphasis upon standards of truth which are independent of the wills of men.*

This first contribution of Christianity is a kind of by-product of its general teaching. Professor Whitehead and others have shown that the possibility of the belief in a dependable world order which underlies modern science is rooted in the medieval world view according to which the mind and will of God gave order to the world. I am suggesting that Christianity may have a similar effect in our time. It teaches first and last that there is a truth which men cannot create but which must be discovered, and which has its origin in the mind of God; that there is a moral rightness which corresponds with the will of God. It is of the utmost importance that, even though men may be skeptical about the Christian revelation of that truth or that moral rightness, they have a sense of the objectivity, the givenness of truth and morality, which goes with the Christian faith. Nothing in all the world is more dangerous or more false than a situation where a thing comes to be regarded as true or right if only a dictator or a minister of propaganda says it often enough.

2. *The Christian must always put loyalty to God as revealed in Christ before loyalty to the state or any earthly power.*

This characteristic of Christianity puts the Christian into a position of irreconcilable opposition to the absolute state. He cannot tolerate without renouncing his religion the claim of the state to regiment the whole of life. He cannot tolerate the attempt of the state to indoctrinate his children with a philosophy of life which is anti-Christian—a philosophy of life which is anti-Christian in its ethics; or in its avowed atheism;

or in its exaltation in idolatrous terms of the state, the leader of the state, the race, or the nation.

Moreover, Christians will find many specific points at which they must put their consciences, guided by the revelation of God's will in Christ, before the expressed will of the state. That will be true where militarism and war are involved. That will be true of the cruel repression of persons which is characteristic of tyrannical states.

In practice Christians have been slow to draw out the full meaning of the independence from the state which is implicit in their religion. They have interpreted the enigmatic saying of Jesus, "Render unto Caesar the things that are Caesar's and unto God the things that are God's," by giving Caesar rather than God the benefit of the doubt. Often, far too often, they have sanctified the will of the state as the will of God. The long story of theories of the divine right of kings and the old habit of emphasizing Paul's words about being loyal to the higher powers as ordained of God are familiar. And even more familiar is the record of the Church in time of war. In the past it has seemed that Christians would take almost anything from a state which did lip service to their religious beliefs no matter how much it flouted their ethics. But that has been a great perversion of what Christianity demands. It is perhaps fortunate at this point that states have arisen which defy the religious beliefs of Christians in order to make Christians once more self-conscious as Christians; but, unless that self-consciousness spreads to ethical issues, it will be of little avail.

3. *Christianity is a universal religion.*

Whatever else is true of Christianity, it is a universal religion. As has been said in earlier chapters, Christianity can only say a solemn "no" to the whole tendency toward exclusive nationalism and racialism which seems to be the peculiar perversion of our times. This tendency, from the point of view of the development of human ideals, is a kind of social infantilism. It goes back to the days before the prophet Amos, for it was he who first saw clearly that God was not merely the God of the people of Israel, but also the God of Syria, Edom, and Tyre—that God was the God of all humanity, the God of an objective order of righteousness and justice. Perhaps when all the present conflicts over ideals are boiled down to their essence we shall find it to be the conflict between every form of particularism (nationalism or racialism) and universalism. In that conflict Christianity may have communism as an ally. There is no doubt but that in the long run universalism will win because an interdependent world organized on a particularistic basis will be reduced to a shambles. But, if Christians are awake to the meaning of their religion they can correct the trends toward particularism before they end in complete tragedy.

4. *The Contradiction between Christianity and War.*

The fact that there is a contradiction between Christianity and war is implied in what has been said about nationalism and economic injustice, which are the chief roots of war. War in itself is not only a futile horror which, on the basis of common sense, is the final condemnation of any social order which creates it, but also it is peculiarly in contradiction to all that Christianity means because of what it makes persons do to persons. There is no more terrific indictment of the practice of Christians in the past than to point out their willingness to accommodate their religion to the war system. One of the real gains since the World War, which the discouraging events of the past few years have not erased, is the development within the Christian Church of a new conscience about war. We are at the beginning of a process in which the warlike Christian nations of the west will find themselves forced to choose between Christianity and war. It is an unconscious tribute to the Christian faith that in one country where militaristic nationalism has gone far cults of race and blood are arising as substitutes for Christianity.

The development of a Christian conscience about war has not been rapid enough to change the habits of all history in a generation. We must admit that we are now caught in a situation in which there seems to be no clear road to the prevention of another large-scale war. It is not inevitable, but only unpredictable events will prevent it. Christianity as such has no political panacea for the prevention of war nor is there any simple answer to the question as to what Christians should do if war does come. There are, however, several things which should be said.

Christians can no longer follow blindly their governments into all wars. This is an application of the general principle that Christians owe their first allegiance to God and to the welfare of the whole human community and not to the state.

There has developed a strong body of Christians who oppose participation in all wars. Many of these would be called "absolute pacifists" in the sense that they reject all organized violence against persons as inherently and inevitably wrong. Others would be called more correctly "pragmatic pacifists," because they base their opposition to war on their belief that no conceivable war would have consequences which would be worth the cost. This second type of pacifism is a relative matter because it is easier to accept it if one lives in America than if one lives in a country which is threatened by invasion. Though neither of these forms of pacifism can in the present situation be regarded as the only Christian position, it is of incalculable importance to have such groups within every nation. They will stand the best chance of being proof against the blinding effect of propaganda and they will, whatever comes, be the salt of sanity in a mad world.

To many Christians complete pacifism seems to have no realistic strategy in the face of actual cases of aggression. Large sections of the Church have come to employ two standards by which participation in war should be tested: Is it a war to defend the territory of a country against actual invasion? Is it a war to implement decisions of a body such as the League of Nations, which represents public law rather than merely a national will? Both of these tests raise serious practical problems, but the effort to discover a middle ground between the sanctification of every war and complete pacifism is an enormous advance in Christian thinking about war.

If another war does come in our time, it will not mean the final defeat of Christianity. It will make it all the clearer that in the long struggle against war Christianity and common sense and ordinary human decency are on the same side. In the disintegration of the world which would follow such a war the existence of an international fellowship of Christians, the roots of which not even war can destroy, would be one of the chief sources of healing and reconstruction. As will be stressed later, for the Church to become a framework which can make such a fellowship effective would be an indispensable contribution to the cause of peace.

5. *The Significance of the Christian Church.*

Thus far in this discussion we have dealt with Christianity mainly as though it were disembodied or embodied only in individual Christians. It is, however, in this context that we can see in a fresh way the significance of the Christian Church. So long as people believed in the early development of a Christian society in the world, except for those who had a high sacramental conception of the Church, it was that developing Christian society which quite largely took the place of the Church in their interest. It is as Christians come to see the degree to which they are living in a world which is alien or hostile that they are thrown together as a Church against the world. Christians, as individuals, are helpless in the face of the problems which we have been discussing.

Before the rôle which the Church can play in our world is described it would be well to pause and deal with one initial difficulty which the word "Church" raises in the minds of many. Is not the Church so divided, so obscurantist in its thinking, so closely tied up with the very forces which Christians must oppose, that it can only be dismissed as a hopeless institution? Such a question is natural if one looks only at a cross section of the existing churches. But, it is in certain trends in the life of the Church that there is real ground for hope. I can but mention four such trends.

The rigid forms of orthodoxy in most denominations have disintegrated, and we have an intellectual awakening in the leadership of the churches in all parts of America which is profoundly modifying the mind of the churches. Almost all of the important theological seminaries, which are the best clue to what the churches are becoming, are now based on the assumption that the content of Christian belief must be brought into relations with the assured results of science. A second change which is going on rapidly is the awakening of the social conscience of the churches. The leadership and many strategic centers, such as theological seminaries and church boards and periodicals, in most of the denominations are committed to the position that Christianity demands drastic changes in the structure of social life. (The policies of the Federal Council of Churches are based on this assumption.) A third change is the rapid increase of coöperation and in some cases of actual union between the churches. A fourth change is the development of a habit of self-criticism in the churches themselves. The existence of innumerable objective surveys of the work of the churches, inspired by the churches themselves but often relentless in their criticisms, is one evidence of this attitude of self-criticism. I urge any reader of these words who lightly dismisses the Church as hopeless because of his experience of one or two specific churches to make an effort to see how far these tendencies are characteristic. *

There are at least two contributions which the Christian Church can make in relation to the problems discussed in this chapter.

(1) The Church is the only organism within a nation which by its very nature must be loyal to a God beyond the state, to humanity beyond the nation, to the Kingdom of God beyond any actual social order. To identify the Church very closely with any state, or nation, or social system is to pervert it beyond recognition as a Christian Church. There are also other institutions which can help to keep the regimentation of the state from being complete. The university should resist the will of the state in the interests of objective truth, although actually the university is more easily suppressed than the Church. In Germany the churches have held out longer against complete regimentation than any other institution and it is significant that the German Protestant churches were seriously handicapped for such an ordeal by the fact that

---

* One book which would have in it most of the necessary material is a symposium recently published entitled, *The Church Through Half a Century*. (Scribners, 1936.)

historically they have been more dependent upon the state than most churches. In America the churches are far better prepared to resist the state both on the issue of their own freedom and on the ethical issues of nationalism, racialism, dictatorship, and war. We cannot be sure that they will necessarily have the strength to win against the state. They have more chance of winning, however, than any other force in American life.

(2) The Church is the only international organism which has real roots in the various nations. There are international institutions which bring together governments in a rather tenuous way. There is some hope in the international labor and radical movements though there is nothing about either labor or radicalism which by its very nature must be international. A church is not a Christian church at all unless its loyalties and outlook are international. In a world which is threatened by disintegration the international church remains the chief hope. As a matter of fact, there is coming into existence a world consciousness among the Protestant churches which can be seen both in the degree to which those churches have strengthened the peace forces in their own countries and by the world movement among Protestants which has its outward and visible signs in the world conferences which are to be held in Oxford and in Edinburgh in the summer of 1937—conferences which are but the continuation of a development begun at the great conferences at Stockholm and Lausanne ten years ago. Let it be said again that we must not suppose that the churches will neces-

sarily be able to turn back the present drift toward war; but in the churches there is developing a force which will count heavily in the long struggle against war.

In this perspective the whole movement in the churches which has gone under the name of "Foreign Missions" assumes a new meaning. Doubtless the missionary movement is at the end of a period, and there must be a great change both in its methods and in the way in which it states its objectives; but the missionary movement is no more than an embodiment of the universalism of Christianity. If Christianity is true in its ideal and in its religious faith, it is true for all the world. If it is to be a power which can unify the life of men on a level deeper than all conflicts it must not be limited to Europe and America. For, in the event of a racial conflict between East and West, if there is no body of common ideals and no common faith, we shall emerge from our present dark period only to enter an age which is even darker.

*   *   *   *   *   *   *   *

There is an old letter, coming from the second century of the life of the Church, the epistle to Diognetus. The unknown writer says of the Christians in his time that "they hold the world together." To his contemporaries those words must have seemed to be absurd enough, but they have turned out to be true. It was Christianity which did hold the world together during a period of disintegration, and it was Christianity which preserved for the future the best in the civilization which collapsed.   In our day, to say that Christianity may hold the world together cannot seem quite so absurd as it did then, but it may be hard enough to believe.   Yet, if Christianity is true and if its truth is the correction for the specific perversions of our time, it is the most solid hope we have in the world and from the perspective of a distant future it may be seen that Christianity has in fact held the world together.

BIBLIOGRAPHY

Aubrey, E. E. *Present Theological Tendencies.* $2.00.
A useful guide to the present situation in religious thought.

Brown, Wm. Adams. *Church and State in Contemporary America.* $2.75.
The best single book for American readers about this problem. Also a very helpful discussion of the social strategy of the Church.

Harkness, Georgia. *The Recovery of Ideals.* $2.00.
A comprehensive treatment of the problems which face modern Christianity.

Hobhouse, L. T. *The Rational Good.* $2.00.
An excellent statement of the rational basis for ethics. Rather difficult.

Horton, W. M. *Realistic Theology.* $2.00.
A constructive statement of Christian faith in the light of the current realistic appraisal of our human situation.

Laidler, H. W. *How America Lives.* 15 cents.
America in the Depression. 15 cents.
Two brief, authoritative handbooks of facts about the economic situation in America.

Laski, H. J. *Communism.* $1.00.
A brief introduction to the thought and program of communism.

Luccock, H. E. *Christian Faith and Economic Change.* $2.00.
A balanced statement of the relation between Christianity and the economic problem. Very readable.

Lyman, E. W. *The Meaning and Truth of Religion.* $3.00.
Probably the best all-round book on the philosophy of religion.

Macmurray, John. *Creative Society.* $1.50.
One of the best attempts to say what Christianity means in relation to communism.

Maritain, Jacques. *True Humanism.* $3.50.
An excellent Roman Catholic discussion of these problems. Objective in the social issues that often divide Catholics and Protestants.

Niebuhr, Reinhold. *Moral Man and Immoral Society.* $2.00.
An Interpretation of Christian Ethics. $2.00.
Niebuhr's two most important books. Difficult but indispensable.

Oldham, J. H. (Editor.) *The Oxford Conference* (Official Report). $2.00.
The most authoritative statements of the attitudes of the leaders of the churches toward the problems with which this book deals.

Tennant, F. R. *Philosophical Theology* (especially Volume 2). $5.00.
The most persuasive statement of the intellectual basis for Christian faith which I know. Very difficult but of great importance.

Van Dusen, H. P. *God in These Times.* $2.00.
A fine diagnosis of the present spiritual situation. Very readable.

Van Dusen and Cavert. *The Church Through Half a Century.* $3.00.
A symposium which contains in most convenient form the material necessary for understanding the contemporary American Church.

FOR DISCUSSION

Outline prepared by Miss Fern Babcock, Secretary of
Southwest Council of Student Christian Associations

Chapter I

CHRISTIANITY AND SECULARISM

WHAT DO WE MEAN BY SECULARISM?

1. What elements in contemporary life are organized as though
God did not exist?

2. How is it possible to do what God wills while denying his existence? Does a social worker who happens to be an atheist do the
will of God in working for better race relations? Does a church goer
who tries "to keep the Negro in his place" do the will of God?

3. Give examples of secularism which makes Gods of human ideals.

4. What difference does it make in the way one lives whether God
exists, or whether human life is the result of blind mechanical processes?

5. Mr. Bennett lists the following roots of secularism in modern life.
List examples of each form of it.

  Leveling life down to those things with which science can deal
  most easily.
  Absorption with things at the expense of reflection.
  Specialization which excludes getting the meaning of life as a
  whole.
  Anti-religious attitudes of radical groups.

WHAT DO WE MEAN BY CHRISTIANITY?

1. To what do we usually give our supreme devotion? Or does our
sense of frustration come from never giving ourselves to anything?
What would it mean to give one's supreme devotion to God?

2. What answers do students give as to the meaning of life, other
than God? Why are these inadequate? How does a "sense of belonging to an order of things give coherence to experience"?

3. Do you ever respond to a good greater than society demands?
Why do you do so? Does the authority of the conscience "come from

beyond ourselves and beyond society," or is the theory that the conscience is merely an accumulation of the past habits of the individual, true?

4. How can God be personal and not be a person? What are the limitations of thinking of him as a person?

5. What are the most striking differences between Jesus and Mussolini? What are the characteristics of Jesus which reveal the nature of God? What did Jesus teach about man's relation to God?

6. Is it the "purpose of God and the spirit of Jesus" that men develop in the world a fellowship which knows no barriers of race or class or nation? How can you reconcile with the purpose of God the following concepts:

"Keep the Negro in his place."

"In a large university where there are all classes of students, it is necessary to have the fraternity system to make the right friends."

"America needs a large navy to protect her foreign interests."

7. Is there something in the moral structure which in the long run makes evil self-defeating? When an individual organizes life around his own selfish ends, what is the result? When society is organized around the desire for profit for a few, what is the result? Is the result accidental or is it in the order of things?

8. Give examples of psychological cases where a personality was crippled by a sense of guilt. Are we the free, fearless persons we might be, or are we harassed by consciousness of our own inadequacies and wrong doing? John Macmurray says that the sense of fear that most people carry comes from the knowledge that one has sinned against society, and that society has it within its power to do them harm. Would a consciousness of the power of God to forgive sins free us of this fear?

9. What are the conditions for deliverance from personal frustration?

10. Are there evils in the world which God does not cause? What are their causes? Is a "community of persons of tested moral worth" more valuable than a community of persons constructed so they could not sin?

11. Contrast the Christian view of man with the current evaluations of psychology about man's possibilities and his handicaps.

12. Why is Christian love a mockery when it is built on anything but a "substructure of economic justice and true equal opportunity in all matters of bread and health and education and environment"? What does equality of opportunity imply?

13. What is the significance of the fact that "there is a movement of life in the world in which God is working most clearly to lift the level of the life of men"?

DIVERGENCE OF CHRISTIANITY FROM COMMUNISM

1. Wherein are the goals of Christianity and communism the same?

2. Why do communists reject religion? Are their reasons valid?

3. What are the dangers which communists share with others in looking upon economic injustice as the sole source of evil?

Chapter II

THE CHRISTIAN ETHIC AND THE MORAL CONFUSION

1. What is the distinction between convention and morality? Is there any deeper reason for morality than that these particular customs have been followed for generations? In what way are moral principles more valid than tabus?

2. What is the evidence that there is "moral structure in the world"? What does Mr. Bennett mean when he says "there is an order of consequences in life which neither individuals nor groups can long defy without bringing obvious punishment on themselves?" Can you give any illustrations of this?

3. What factors in the structure of life make nationalism and racialism evil? How does the class consciousness of communism differ from the other two forms of group egoism?

4. Moderns have laughed at their elders' counsel concerning personal discipline. Is it necessary for an interesting, productive life? Why?

5. Why is integrity necessary to society? How does the lack of integrity react upon the individual?

6. "A part of the protest against conventional morals arises out of this very hatred of sham which is one of the sound things in our civilization." What elements in conventional morality are shams? What elements of conventional morality are rooted in the structure of life? How do conventions come to be?

7. In what way are the two principles of democracy, government resting on the consent of the governed and freedom of expression for minority groups, demanded by the structure of life? What is the consequence of denying these principles?

8. Does monogamy provide the best relationship between the sexes? Why?

9. What elements does Christian morality have in common with ordinary morality? What is distinctive in the Christian ethic?

Chapter III
CHRISTIANITY AND THE ECONOMIC ORDER

1. By and large, is the economic system in America fair? Do the deserving have their basic needs met?

2. Is any group of people responsible for the present injustice? How did America change from a pioneer country where each man owned his home, to the present inequality?

3. What criticisms do economists make of capitalism?

4. Evaluate the three moral criticisms which Mr. Bennett says Christians make of capitalism:

The staggering degree of inequality which capitalism permits. What are the spiritual effects of too much wealth on the rich? Of too little wealth on the poor? Why is equality a basic Christian principle?

The premium capitalism puts on selfishness and deception. How can Christians who believe in the way of love justify capitalism in its appeal to the acquisitive nature of man? How much deception does capitalism foster?

The increasing concentration of economic power. Why is the concentration of power bad? Can the privileged be trusted to decide what is to the best interest of those without privilege? How does the concentration of power make people afraid? Why does Mr. Bennett say that bitterness against injustice is more wholesome and constructive than fear?

5. What is meant by the statement that a Christian is forced to lead a double life in living off the exploitation of the workers and in living in relative privilege side by side with desperate need? Why must a Christian work for structural changes in the economic system? What does "structural change" imply?

6. Can any form of economic order be deduced from Christianity? If not, what is the function of Christianity in delivering us from economic exploitation?

7. What is the Christian meaning of the word "equality"? Why does Mr. Bennett say that the denial of equality of opportunity is not only immoral, but blasphemous?

8. Is poverty inevitable? Do you believe that it is possible to maintain all families in America on a standard of living equal to $2,000 to $5,000 per year?

9. What was Jesus' conception of the relation between the spiritual and the physical aspects of life? To what extent is Christianity a materialistic religion?

10. Did Jesus condemn wealth? For what reasons?

11. Does social change come when people are controlled by Christian ideals? Why does Mr. Bennett say Christians must cooperate with social and political movements? Why does he say that the church must never become identified with any one movement? What is the responsibility of the church in economic change?

Chapter IV
CHRISTIANITY AND THE NEW TYRANNY

1. What is the meaning of the phrase "totalitarian state"? How does the totalitarian state claim the whole of life? Why is it wrong for the state to be the final arbiter in all personal decisions? In what ways does modern science make tyranny more complete than tyranny has been in history?

2. Have you heard speakers point to the dictatorships in Europe and imply that it was only a matter of time until the same thing comes in America? What factors in the American situation are different from the situation in Germany, Italy, or Russia? What factors in America make dictatorship a possibility, even though a remote one?

3. Evaluate each of the contributions of Christianity which Mr. Bennett says may halt the trend toward increased nationalism, tyranny, and war?

Christianity keeps alive the emphasis upon standards of truth which are independent of the wills of men. Can any one dictator see the will of God as clearly as can many Christians in all parts of the earth? How do Christians discover the moral rightness in the world?

The Christian must always put loyalty to God as revealed in Christ before loyalty to the state or to any earthly power. Why? What demands of the state might be in conflict with loyalty to God?

Christianity is a universal religion. What does this imply?

The contradiction between Christianity and War. Is all international warfare morally wrong? How valid are the two standards by which participation in war should be tested by a Christian?

The significance of the Christian Church. What was the significance of the early Christian Church? What could be its significance in establishing a universal community today? What are the hopeful trends in the Church today? How can Christian missions contribute to the universal community?

4. How can you participate in the work of the Church in "holding the world together"? How can you function in the vocation which you have chosen in this supremely significant task?